INTRODU

Hey Swifties! Are you ready to dive into the wonderful world of Taylor Swift? This book is packed with amazing and fun facts about your favorite superstar that will make you love her even more! Some of these facts you might already know, but others will surprise and delight you.

Did you know Taylor loves playing board games with her friends? Or that she writes lyrics on her arms during concerts like secret tattoos? She was the first female artist to have an album debut at number one on the Billboard 200 with "Red." How cool is that?

This book is filled with stories about Taylor's life, from hosting Halloween parties for her fans to writing letters to herself about her dreams. You'll learn about her passion for interior design and how she credits her fans for her success.

So, grab your favorite snack, get cozy, and join us on this exciting journey to learn all about Taylor Swift. Let's see how many of these fun facts you already know and which ones will become your new favorites!

1
TAYLOR IS A SAGITTARIUS

Taylor's birthday is December 13th, making her a Sagittarius, known for being adventurous and optimistic. She was born in Reading, Pennsylvania, a town famous for its scenic beauty and historical landmarks. Growing up in this picturesque place gave her a lot of inspiration for her early music. Her parents, Andrea and Scott Swift, were delighted to welcome her as their second child. Every year, she celebrates her birthday with loved ones, often in a cozy and festive way.

2
NAMED AFTER JAMES TAYLOR

Taylor's parents admired the musician James Taylor so much that they named their daughter after him, hoping she would inherit his musical talent. James Taylor himself has recognized this honor and has even performed with her. Taylor's name is a constant tribute to her parents' love for music and their hopes for her future. It's a meaningful connection that set the tone for her own incredible journey in music. Naming her after such a legendary artist was a special touch by her parents.

3
SHE GREW UP ON A XMAS TREE FARM

Taylor's childhood was magical, living on a Christmas tree farm in Pennsylvania. She remembers helping her family with the farm work, especially during the holiday season when the farm was busiest. This unique upbringing gave her a love for the outdoors and a strong work ethic. Taylor even wrote a nostalgic song about it called "Christmas Tree Farm," which describes the joy and magic of her childhood home. The farm's festive and hardworking atmosphere left a lasting impression on her.

4
WROTE A NOVEL
AT AGE 12

Even as a young girl, Taylor had a vivid imagination and loved storytelling. At 12 years old, she wrote a novel titled "A Girl Named Girl," showing her early talent for writing. Though it was never published, it demonstrated her creative spirit and passion for creating characters and stories. This early experience helped her develop the skills she would later use in her songwriting. Writing a novel at such a young age was just the beginning of her literary journey.

5
MOVED TO
NASHVILLE AT 14

At just 14 years old, Taylor made the brave decision to move to Nashville, Tennessee, known as the heart of country music. This big move was all about chasing her dream of becoming a singer. It was a huge step for someone so young, but she was determined and passionate about her music. She spent countless hours writing songs and performing at local venues. Her hard work and dedication soon paid off, setting her on the path to stardom.

6

HER FIRST SINGLE WAS "TIM MCGRAW"

Taylor's first big hit was a song called "Tim McGraw," released in 2006. This song is about summer love and memories tied to Tim McGraw's music. It quickly caught the attention of country music fans and made people notice her incredible talent. The success of "Tim McGraw" marked the beginning of her amazing career in music. It was the first step in her journey to becoming a superstar.

7
"SPEAK NOW" WRITTEN BY HERSELF

Taylor is not just an amazing singer, but also a talented songwriter. She wrote every single song on her "Speak Now" album all by herself. This album is full of personal stories and emotions, showcasing her incredible ability to connect with her fans through her music. Writing an entire album alone is a big accomplishment and shows how gifted she is. Her fans love the honesty and depth in her songs.

8
USED MYSPACE TO GET FANS

Before Instagram and TikTok, there was Myspace, and Taylor used it to connect with her fans in a unique way. She shared her music and personal stories, making her fans feel really close to her. It was a smart move that helped her build a strong and loyal fan base early in her career. Using Myspace set her apart from other country artists at the time. It showed how savvy and forward-thinking she was even as a young artist.

9
FAVORITE DESSERT IS CHEESECAKE

Taylor loves cheesecake, which is creamy, sweet, and absolutely delicious. It's her go-to dessert for celebrations and special occasions. She enjoys both making and eating this delightful treat. Sometimes, she even shares her homemade cheesecake with friends and fans. It's just one of the many ways she connects with her loved ones through food.

10
SHE COLLECTS ANTIQUE DOORKNOBS

One of Taylor's quirky hobbies is collecting old, unique doorknobs. She finds these antique treasures fascinating and loves the history behind them. These doorknobs add a vintage charm to her home decor. Collecting doorknobs is an unusual but fun hobby that reflects her eclectic taste. It's a small but interesting detail that makes her home special and personal.

11
FEAR OF
SEA URCHINS

Taylor has a deep fear of sea urchins. She thinks of them as underwater landmines because stepping on one can be painful and even dangerous. This fear makes her cautious when swimming in the ocean. Despite her love for the beach, she always watches her step in the water. It's a quirky but serious fear she often talks about.

12
NO TATTOOS

Taylor doesn't have any tattoos due to her fear of needles. While many celebrities sport tattoos, she prefers to express herself through her music and fashion. Her aversion to needles is so strong that she avoids getting inked altogether. This decision makes her unique among her peers. Her style remains ink-free and true to herself.

13
LUCKY NUMBER 13

Taylor's lucky number is 13, which she considers very special. She often writes it on her hand during concerts for good luck. To her, the number brings positivity and success, even though many people see it as unlucky. Her connection to the number started early in her career and continues today. It's a fun and personal superstition she embraces wholeheartedly.

14
AKA NILS SJÖBERG

Taylor co-wrote the hit song "This Is What You Came For" under the pseudonym Nils Sjöberg. She chose to use a different name to keep her involvement a secret initially. The song, performed by Calvin Harris and Rihanna, became a huge hit. Using a pseudonym allowed her to experiment with songwriting anonymously. Later, she revealed her contribution, surprising many fans.

15
LEARNING TO DRIVE

Taylor learned to drive from her mom and doesn't have a formal driver's license. Instead of going through a traditional driving school, she practiced on her family's farm. This unique experience added a personal touch to her driving skills. Her mom played a significant role in teaching her. It's one of the many ways her family has supported her.

16
SUMMER HOUSE

Taylor owns a beautiful eight-bedroom summer house in Watch Hill, Rhode Island. This house is famous for hosting her legendary Fourth of July parties. It's a place where she can relax and spend time with friends and family. The house offers stunning views and plenty of space for gatherings. It's her perfect getaway spot.

17
CAT LOVER

Taylor has three adorable cats named Meredith Grey, Olivia Benson, and Benjamin Button. These cats are named after her favorite TV and movie characters. They often appear in her social media posts and even in some of her music videos. Her love for cats is well-known among her fans. The trio brings her joy and companionship.

18
CELEBRITY FRIENDS

Taylor is friends with many celebrities, including Selena Gomez and Ed Sheeran. They often support each other's music and projects. Their friendships are well-documented through social media and public appearances. Taylor's circle of friends includes artists from various genres. These relationships highlight her friendly and supportive nature.

19
FEAR OF SPIDERS AND BEETLES

Like many people, Taylor has a strong fear of spiders and beetles. Despite her brave persona on stage, these creepy crawlies give her the heebie-jeebies. She often talks about this fear in interviews, making her relatable to fans. It's one of her biggest personal fears. Even superstars have things that scare them!

20
TAYLOR THE STOCKBROKER?

Before choosing music, Taylor considered becoming a stockbroker, inspired by her grandmother. Her grandmother worked in finance, and Taylor admired her career. However, her love for music eventually won out. She decided to follow her passion, which led to her incredible career in the music industry. It's a reminder that our dreams can change as we grow.

21
TRAILER IN
MUSIC VIDEO

In her "You Need to Calm Down" music video, Taylor used her own trailer. She bought it specifically for the video to add a personal touch. The colorful, fun trailer perfectly matched the video's vibrant theme. Fans loved seeing this glimpse of her personal style. It shows how much she enjoys being hands-on with her projects.

22
SECRET MESSAGES IN LYRICS

Taylor has a special code where she hides secret messages in her album lyrics. By capitalizing certain letters in the printed lyrics, she spells out hidden words and clues. Fans eagerly decode these messages to find out more about her inspirations and stories behind the songs. This interactive element makes her albums even more engaging. It's a fun way she connects with her audience.

23
HOMESCHOOLING DIPLOMA

Despite her busy music career, Taylor didn't miss out on her education. She was homeschooled and received her high school diploma this way. Balancing schoolwork with her rising fame was challenging, but she managed it with determination. Her dedication to education shows how important learning is to her. It's an inspiring example for young fans.

24
LOVE FOR BAKING

Taylor loves to cook and bake, often whipping up treats for her friends and fans. She's known for making delicious cookies and cakes. Baking is one of her favorite ways to relax and show appreciation to her loved ones. She sometimes shares her recipes, bringing joy to many kitchens. It's a sweet way she spreads happiness.

25
CORN MAZE TRIBUTE

In 2018, a farm in Maryland honored Taylor with a giant corn maze designed to look like her face. This creative tribute celebrated her impact and popularity. Fans flocked to the maze to navigate through the fields shaped like their favorite star. It was a fun and unique way to show appreciation for her music. Taylor was thrilled and touched by this unusual honor.

26
"ROMEO AND JULIET" INSPIRATION

Taylor wrote her hit song "Love Story" inspired by William Shakespeare's "Romeo and Juliet." She gave the classic tale a happy ending, different from the original tragic story. This song became one of her most beloved hits, resonating with fans everywhere. It's a modern twist on a timeless romance. The song's success highlights her talent for storytelling through music.

27
FIRST
NUMBER-ONE HIT

Taylor's first number-one hit on the Billboard Hot 100 was "We Are Never Ever Getting Back Together." This catchy breakup anthem became an instant favorite. Fans loved its upbeat melody and relatable lyrics. The song marked a significant milestone in her career, proving her crossover appeal. It showcased her ability to create hits in both country and pop genres.

28
BEST-SELLING
ALBUM "FEARLESS"

"Fearless" is Taylor's best-selling album, featuring many hit songs like "Love Story" and "You Belong with Me." This album won several awards and solidified her status as a top artist. Fans adore the heartfelt lyrics and catchy melodies. "Fearless" remains a defining album in her career. Its success opened many doors for her future projects.

29
TIME'S "100 MOST INFLUENTIAL PEOPLE"

Time magazine has named Taylor one of the "100 Most Influential People" multiple times. This honor recognizes her impact on music, culture, and society. Taylor's influence extends beyond her music to her philanthropy and advocacy. She inspires millions with her actions and words. Being on this list highlights her global significance.

30
11 GRAMMY AWARDS

Taylor has won an impressive 11 Grammy Awards, celebrating her musical talent and achievements. Each Grammy win is a special moment in her career. These awards recognize her excellence in songwriting, performance, and production. Winning multiple Grammys showcases her versatility and dedication to her craft. It's a testament to her hard work and artistry.

31
GUEST APPEARANCE ON CSI

Taylor made a guest appearance on the TV show CSI in 2009. She played a rebellious teen named Haley Jones, who met a tragic end. It was a chance for her to showcase her acting skills. The role was different from her music persona and she enjoyed the challenge. Fans loved seeing Taylor in a new light.

32
FILM DEBUT IN "VALENTINE'S DAY"

Taylor made her film debut in the movie "Valentine's Day" in 2010. She played a bubbly high school student named Felicia. Acting alongside stars like Julia Roberts and Bradley Cooper was a thrilling experience for her. She brought her charm and humor to the role. It was fun to see her transition from music to acting.

33
VOICED AUDREY IN "THE LORAX"

Taylor lent her voice to Audrey, a character in the animated film "The Lorax." The movie is based on Dr. Seuss's beloved book about environmental conservation. Taylor's character dreams of seeing a real tree in a world without them. She enjoyed bringing Audrey's hopeful spirit to life. Fans appreciated hearing her voice in a family-friendly film.

34
DATED JOE JONAS

Taylor once dated Joe Jonas for a few months in 2008. Their relationship was short but memorable. They were both rising stars at the time and their relationship caught a lot of media attention. Taylor even wrote a song, "Forever & Always," about their breakup. Despite the brief romance, they both moved on and continued their successful careers.

35
PRIVATE JET AND HANGAR

Taylor owns a Dassault Falcon 900 private jet. This luxurious jet allows her to travel comfortably for her tours and personal trips. She also has an airport hangar at Nashville International Airport to house her jet. Owning a private jet gives her the flexibility to manage her busy schedule. It's one of the perks of being a global superstar.

36
"SHAKE IT OFF"
SUCCESS

Her song "Shake It Off" became a huge hit and reached number one on the Billboard Hot 100. This upbeat anthem encourages listeners to ignore negativity and just enjoy life. Its catchy melody and fun lyrics made it a favorite among fans. The music video, featuring Taylor dancing in various styles, added to its popularity. It remains one of her most iconic songs.

37
MOST STREAMED SONG

Taylor's most streamed song on Spotify is "I Don't Want to Live Forever," a collaboration with Zayn Malik. The song was part of the Fifty Shades Darker soundtrack and has been streamed over a billion times. Its sultry vibe and emotional lyrics captivated listeners. Collaborating with Zayn brought a new dynamic to her music. The song's success shows her versatility as an artist.

38
"BLANK SPACE" YOUTUBE VIEWS

"Blank Space" is her most-viewed music video on YouTube with over 3.3 billion views. The video portrays Taylor in a mansion, going through the highs and lows of a fictional relationship. Its dramatic and humorous take on her public image was a hit. Fans loved the clever lyrics and stunning visuals. The video's massive view count reflects its enduring popularity.

39

AMERICAN MUSIC AWARDS

Taylor holds the record for the most American Music Awards won by a female artist. She has received numerous AMAs throughout her career, highlighting her impact on the music industry. These awards are based on fan votes, showing her strong connection with her audience. Each win is a testament to her talent and popularity. Taylor's AMA achievements are part of her impressive legacy.

40
YOUNGEST ARTIST SIGNED BY SONY/ATV

At just 14, Taylor was the youngest artist ever signed by the Sony/ATV Music publishing house. This early recognition of her songwriting talent set the stage for her future success. Signing with such a prestigious company was a big achievement. It marked the beginning of her professional music career. Her youthful determination and talent shone through from the start.

41
DATED HARRY STYLES

Taylor Swift dated Harry Styles from late 2012 to January 2013. Their relationship was highly publicized, and they were often seen together at various events. Taylor wrote songs like "Style" and "Out of the Woods" about their time together. Their short romance remains one of the most talked-about celebrity pairings. Despite the breakup, both have continued to respect each other's work.

42
CLOSE WITH FAMILY

Taylor has a strong bond with her family, often mentioning them in interviews. Her parents, Andrea and Scott, and her younger brother, Austin, are very supportive of her career. They often travel with her on tours and attend her award shows. Taylor credits her family's support as a key factor in her success. They have always been her biggest fans.

43
FAVORITE BOOK

Taylor's favorite book is "To Kill a Mockingbird" by Harper Lee. She has mentioned that the themes of justice and empathy deeply resonate with her. The book's strong moral lessons influenced her perspective on life. She admires the character of Atticus Finch for his wisdom and integrity. This classic novel remains a source of inspiration for her.

44
BOOK OF POETRY

Taylor has her own book of poetry, showcasing her love for writing beyond music. Her poetry reflects her personal thoughts and experiences. It's another way for her to connect with fans on a deeper level. Writing poetry helps her express emotions and creativity. It's a hobby she enjoys alongside songwriting.

45

PRESTIGIOUS PERFORMANCES

Taylor has performed at prestigious events worldwide, including the Grammy Awards. Her performances are known for their energy and creativity. She often surprises audiences with unique stage setups and special guests. These high-profile performances have cemented her status as a top entertainer. Fans eagerly anticipate her live shows for unforgettable experiences.

46
GIVES TO CHARITY

Taylor has donated millions to various charitable causes, including education and disaster relief. She is known for her generosity and commitment to helping those in need. Her donations have supported schools, libraries, and emergency response efforts. Taylor often uses her platform to raise awareness for important issues. Her philanthropy is a significant part of her legacy.

47
"1989" ALBUM TRANSITION

Taylor's album "1989" marked a significant transition to pop music. The album was a departure from her country roots and embraced a more polished pop sound. Songs like "Shake It Off" and "Blank Space" became huge hits. This successful shift expanded her fan base and showcased her versatility. "1989" won several awards and remains one of her most popular albums.

48
GUINNESS WORLD RECORDS

Taylor holds 101 Guinness World Records, highlighting her achievements in music. These records recognize milestones like album sales, streaming numbers, and award wins. Each record is a testament to her impact and popularity. Taylor's accomplishments continue to set new standards in the industry. Her records inspire aspiring musicians worldwide.

49
SIX CONCERT TOURS

Taylor has had six major concert tours, starting with the Fearless Tour. Each tour features elaborate stage designs, costumes, and performances. Her tours are known for their storytelling and theatrical elements. Fans travel from all over the world to see her live. Each tour is a celebration of her music and connection with her audience.

50
FAVORITE
COLOR

Taylor's favorite color is purple. She often incorporates this color into her outfits and stage designs. Purple represents creativity, mystery, and magic, which aligns with her artistic personality. Fans often wear purple to her concerts to show their support. It's a small but fun way to connect with her.

51
GIFTS FROM FANS ROOM

Taylor has a special room in her house dedicated to gifts from fans. This room is filled with letters, artwork, and other thoughtful presents sent by her admirers. It shows how much she appreciates their support. Keeping these gifts allows her to feel connected to her fans even when she's not performing. It's a heartfelt way to cherish the bond she has with them.

52
ANDREW LLOYD WEBBER'S PIANO

Taylor owns a piano that once belonged to the famous composer Andrew Lloyd Webber. This special piano adds a touch of musical history to her home. Playing on such a legendary instrument is inspiring for Taylor. It represents her deep love for music and songwriting. This piece of history is a treasured item in her collection.

53
SELF-PROCLAIMED NOVELIST

At the age of 12, Taylor wrote a novel titled "A Girl Named Girl." While many kids were playing outside, she was busy crafting stories. Her parents still have the manuscript, and Taylor has mentioned it fondly in interviews. This early love for writing translated into her songwriting talents. Who knows? Maybe one day she'll publish it for the world to read!

54
COLLABORATIONS
WITH ARTISTS

Taylor has collaborated with numerous artists, including Kendrick Lamar and Ed Sheeran. These collaborations bring different styles and influences to her music. Working with diverse artists allows her to experiment and grow creatively. Each collaboration is unique and often leads to chart-topping hits. Fans love seeing her team up with their favorite musicians.

55
CMA ENTERTAINER OF THE YEAR AWARD

Taylor was the youngest artist to win the CMA Award for Entertainer of the Year. This prestigious award recognized her impact on the country music industry. Winning at such a young age was a significant milestone in her career. It validated her hard work and talent. The award remains one of her proudest achievements.

56
FAMOUS SQUAD

Taylor has a close-knit group of friends known as her "squad." This group includes celebrities like Selena Gomez, Karlie Kloss, and Gigi Hadid. They often support each other's projects and appear in each other's social media posts. Taylor's squad symbolizes friendship and female empowerment. Fans admire their strong bond and supportive nature.

57
APPEARANCE ON "NEW GIRL"

Taylor made a surprise appearance in an episode of the TV show "New Girl." She played Elaine, a guest at a wedding, in the show's season finale. Her cameo was well-received and added a fun twist to the episode. Taylor's acting skills shone through, delighting fans and viewers.
It was a memorable TV moment.

58
PLATINUM ALBUM "SPEAK NOW"

Taylor was the first female artist to have an album go platinum on its first day of release with "Speak Now." This incredible achievement showcased her immense popularity and fan support. The album features many personal and heartfelt songs written solely by Taylor. Its immediate success solidified her status as a music powerhouse. The album remains a favorite among her fans.

59
KNITTING GIFTS

Taylor is an avid knitter and often makes handmade gifts for her friends. She finds knitting relaxing and enjoys creating personalized items. Her friends cherish these special gifts, knowing they were made with love. Taylor's knitting skills add a personal touch to her friendships. It's a creative and thoughtful hobby that she loves.

60
VINTAGE DRESSES AND JEWELRY

Taylor has a collection of vintage dresses and jewelry. She enjoys finding unique and stylish pieces from different eras. These items add a classic and elegant touch to her wardrobe. Her love for vintage fashion reflects her appreciation for history and timeless beauty. Fans often admire her retro-inspired looks.

61
LOVES GARDENING

Taylor enjoys gardening and has a beautiful vegetable garden at her home. She finds peace and joy in planting and taking care of her plants. Growing her own vegetables and flowers allows her to connect with nature. She often shares her gardening adventures with friends and family, bringing fresh produce to the table. It's a relaxing hobby that keeps her connected with nature.

62
MOVIE SOUNDTRACKS

Taylor has written songs for several movie soundtracks, including "The Hunger Games." Her song "Safe & Sound," featuring The Civil Wars, was part of the soundtrack and received critical acclaim. The hauntingly beautiful track added depth to the movie's atmosphere. Collaborating on movie soundtracks allows her to explore different themes and emotions. Fans love hearing her voice in these cinematic projects.

63
FOUR MILLION-PLUS SELLING ALBUMS

Taylor was the first artist to have four albums sell over one million copies in their first week. This incredible achievement includes her albums "Speak Now," "Red," "1989," and "Reputation." Each album showcased her growth and versatility as an artist. Her record-setting success highlights her strong connection with fans. This milestone solidified her place in music history.

64
NAMING GUITARS

Taylor has a habit of naming her guitars. Each guitar is special to her and has its own unique name, giving them character. Naming her guitars makes them feel like old friends. This personal touch shows her deep connection to her music. Her fans love hearing the stories behind each guitar's name.

65
WOMAN OF THE DECADE

Taylor was the first woman to win the Billboard Music Award for Woman of the Decade. This award recognized her incredible achievements and influence in the music industry over ten years. Her hard work, talent, and dedication to her craft earned her this prestigious honor. It highlighted her as a trailblazer for women in music. This accolade celebrates her lasting impact on the industry.

66
GIRL SCOUT

Taylor was a Girl Scout growing up. This experience helped shape her values of community and leadership. She often speaks fondly of her time as a Scout, where she learned important life skills. The lessons she learned have influenced her charitable efforts and connection with fans. Being a Girl Scout was an important part of her childhood.

67
HOME RECORDING STUDIO

Taylor has a home recording studio where she produces much of her music. This private space allows her to experiment and create freely. Having her own studio means she can work on her music anytime inspiration strikes. It's a sanctuary for her creativity. Many of her hit songs were born in this personal studio.

68
JOURNALING HABIT

Taylor has kept diaries since she was a child. Journaling is a way for her to express her thoughts and reflect on her experiences. These diaries have helped her develop her songwriting skills. Writing regularly allows her to process her emotions and craft heartfelt lyrics. Her journals are a cherished part of her personal history.

69
HANDWRITTEN NOTES TO FANS

Taylor often sends handwritten notes to her fans. These notes are her way of showing appreciation and staying connected with her supporters. Fans treasure these personal messages, which make them feel special. Taylor's thoughtfulness in writing these notes highlights her genuine care for her fans. It's one of the many ways she gives back to her community.

70
PERSONAL TRAINER AND SOLO WORKOUTS

While Taylor has a personal trainer, she prefers to work out on her own. She enjoys activities like running, yoga, and cardio exercises. Working out helps her stay healthy and manage stress. She finds solo workouts to be a great time to clear her mind and stay focused. Staying active is important for her overall well-being.

71
CAMEO ON "THE VOICE"

Taylor once had a cameo in an episode of "The Voice." She enjoyed the experience of mentoring contestants and sharing her music industry knowledge. Her appearance was a hit with fans and contestants alike. She brought her unique insights and charisma to the show. It was a fun way for her to connect with aspiring artists and audiences.

72
SURPRISING FANS

Taylor has a habit of surprising her fans with personal visits and gifts. She has shown up at bridal showers, sent personalized holiday cards, and even invited fans to her home for secret listening sessions. These surprises make her fans feel special and appreciated. It's one of the many ways she shows gratitude for their support. Her unexpected appearances have created unforgettable memories for many.

73
COLLECTS
RARE BOOKS

Taylor has a collection of rare books. She loves finding unique and vintage editions of her favorite stories. This hobby reflects her deep appreciation for literature and storytelling. Collecting rare books allows her to enjoy the physical beauty and history of literature. It's a quiet and intellectual pastime that she finds fulfilling.

74
BILLBOARD'S WOMAN OF THE YEAR TWICE

Taylor was the first woman to be named Billboard's Woman of the Year twice. This prestigious honor highlights her influence and success in the music industry. Winning it twice showcases her continued relevance and impact over the years. It celebrates her achievements and contributions to music. Her repeated recognition underscores her status as a leading artist of her generation.

75
HOME LIBRARY WITH OVER 500 BOOKS

Taylor has a home library with over 500 books. This extensive collection includes novels, poetry, and historical texts. She enjoys spending time reading and expanding her knowledge. The library is a cozy retreat where she can relax and immerse herself in different worlds. It's a testament to her love of reading and learning.

76
DOODLES IN NOTEBOOKS

Taylor has a habit of doodling in her notebooks. She often draws little pictures and designs while writing lyrics or brainstorming ideas. These doodles add a personal and creative touch to her work. It's a fun way for her to express herself visually. Her notebooks are filled with these unique and spontaneous artworks.

77
FAMOUS CHOCOLATE CHIP COOKIES RECIPE

Taylor has a special recipe for chocolate chip cookies that she often shares with fans. Baking is one of her favorite ways to relax and show appreciation for her friends. Her cookies are famous among her circle and have been featured in interviews. Sharing the recipe allows fans to enjoy a taste of her homemade treats. It's a sweet way she connects with others.

78
THANK-YOU NOTES TO RADIO DJS

Taylor is known for writing thank-you notes to radio DJs who play her music. This thoughtful gesture shows her appreciation for their support. Her handwritten notes are a personal touch that sets her apart. These notes have made a positive impression on many in the music industry. It's one of the many ways she builds strong relationships within the industry.

79
PRANKED
ED SHEERAN

Taylor once played a prank on her friend Ed Sheeran by putting his phone number on a poster at her concert. The poster read, "Call Ed," and it led to a hilarious influx of calls for Ed. This playful joke showed her fun-loving side and sense of humor. Ed took it in stride, and it became a memorable moment in their friendship. Fans loved seeing this light-hearted interaction between the two stars.

80

VINTAGE TYPEWRITER COLLECTION

Taylor has a collection of vintage typewriters. She loves the charm and history of these classic machines. Typing on them adds a nostalgic feel to her writing process. This collection reflects her appreciation for vintage items and the art of writing. Each typewriter holds a special place in her heart and home.

81
HOME DECOR WITH MEMORIES

Taylor has a habit of decorating her home with memorabilia from her tours. Her house is like a gallery of her career, filled with posters, awards, and costumes. These items remind her of all the fun and hard work from her concerts. It's a personal touch that makes her home feel cozy and special. Fans would love to see the amazing memories Taylor has displayed.

82
VINYL RECORD
COLLECTION

Taylor has a collection of vintage vinyl records. She loves the classic sound and the nostalgia they bring. Her collection includes albums from many different artists and genres. Listening to vinyl records is a relaxing hobby for her. It's a way for Taylor to enjoy music just like her fans enjoy her songs.

83
PHOTOGRAPHY PASSION

Taylor has a passion for photography and often takes her own promotional photos. She enjoys capturing moments and creating visually appealing images. Photography allows her to express her creativity in another medium. Some of her favorite shots are used in her album artwork and social media posts. It's a hobby that complements her artistic career.

84
BAKING COOKIES BEFORE ALBUMS

Taylor has a habit of baking cookies before releasing a new album. She finds baking to be a calming activity amidst the excitement of an album launch. The delicious aroma of freshly baked cookies fills her home, adding to the joyful atmosphere. She often shares these treats with her team and friends as a sweet way to celebrate. This tradition adds a personal touch to her album release process.

85
CRASHING A FAN'S BRIDAL SHOWER

Taylor once crashed a fan's bridal shower, creating an unforgettable moment. She surprised the bride-to-be with a personal visit and gifts, showing her appreciation for her dedicated fan. The surprise visit was heartfelt and brought joy to everyone present. Taylor's gesture demonstrated her genuine care for her fans. It's one of the many ways she connects personally with her audience.

86
COLLECTION OF RARE BOOKS

Taylor has a collection of rare books. She loves finding unique and vintage editions of her favorite stories. This hobby reflects her deep appreciation for literature and storytelling. Collecting rare books allows her to enjoy the physical beauty and history of literature. It's a quiet and intellectual pastime that she finds fulfilling.

87
BOARD GAME ENTHUSIAST

Taylor loves playing board games with her friends. It's one of her favorite ways to unwind and have fun. Whether it's a classic game like Monopoly or something more strategic, she loves the friendly competition. Playing board games allows her to bond with friends in a relaxed setting. It's a simple yet enjoyable pastime that brings joy and laughter.

88
LYRIC TATTOOS

During concerts, Taylor has a habit of writing lyrics on her arms. These are often her favorite lines from songs, which she scribbles with a marker. It's her unique way of sharing personal messages and inspiration with her fans. The writing on her arm also serves as a cool, temporary tattoo that changes with each performance. It's like a secret code between Taylor and her audience.

89
CHART-TOPPING
"RED"

Taylor was the first female artist to have an album debut at number one on the Billboard 200 with "Red." This album features some of her biggest hits like "We Are Never Ever Getting Back Together." Fans loved its mix of pop and country sounds. Its success showed how Taylor's music could cross genres and appeal to a wide audience. "Red" becoming number one was a huge achievement and made history.

90
HALLOWEEN
HOSTESS

Taylor once hosted a Halloween party for her fans at her home. She loves Halloween and enjoys dressing up in fun costumes. Inviting her fans to celebrate with her made the holiday extra special. The party was full of spooky decorations, yummy treats, and lots of laughter. Taylor's Halloween bash was a night to remember for everyone who attended.

91
RECORD-BREAKING ALBUMS

She was the first artist to have three albums sell over one million copies in their first week. This incredible feat includes her albums "Speak Now," "Red," and "1989." Each release showcased her growth and versatility as an artist. Selling so many albums so quickly showed just how much her fans loved her music. It's a record that highlights her superstar status.

92
INSPIRATIONAL PLAYLIST

Taylor has a special playlist of songs that inspire her. These are tunes that give her energy and ideas for her own music. She listens to them when she needs a creative boost. Sharing this playlist with fans would let them see a bit of her musical influences. It's a fun way to connect with her through the music that she loves.

93
HIDDEN MESSAGES

She often includes hidden messages in her album artwork. Fans love finding these secret clues and deciphering their meanings. It's like a treasure hunt with each new album. These messages can be anything from hidden lyrics to special thank-yous. It makes listening to her music even more exciting and interactive.

94
BAKING PIES FOR NEIGHBORS

Taylor has a habit of baking pies for her neighbors. She enjoys the process of making delicious treats from scratch. Sharing these pies is her way of spreading kindness and building community. Her neighbors always look forward to her tasty surprises. It's a sweet tradition that shows her generous spirit.

95
BLACK DOG
SWAMPED

The Black Dog is a pub in South London. The pub is now visited by thousands of Swifties every month ever since it was revealed that it's the place that Taylor refers to in the 17th track of The Tortured Poets Department.

96
AWARDS ROOM

Taylor has a special room in her house dedicated to her awards. This room is filled with trophies, plaques, and other honors she has received. It's a space that showcases her many accomplishments. Having a dedicated room for her awards reminds her of all the milestones she has reached. It's an inspiring sight for any visitor.

97
RARE STAMP COLLECTION

Taylor has a collection of rare stamps. She enjoys the history and art of these small but detailed pieces. Collecting stamps is a hobby that she finds both relaxing and fascinating. Each stamp in her collection tells a story from different parts of the world. It's a unique way for her to explore history and culture.

98
LETTERS TO HERSELF

Taylor often writes letters to herself about her goals and dreams. This practice helps her stay focused and motivated. Writing these letters allows her to reflect on her progress and set new aspirations. It's a personal tradition that keeps her grounded. Her letters are a way to connect with her future self and track her journey.

99
INTERIOR DESIGN PASSION

She has a passion for interior design and decorated her homes herself. Taylor loves creating beautiful and comfortable spaces. Her sense of style is reflected in every room of her houses. She enjoys choosing colors, furniture, and decorations that make her feel at home. Interior design is another way she expresses her creativity.

100
FAN APPRECIATION

Taylor has a special place in her heart for her fans and often credits them for her success. She knows that without their support, she wouldn't be where she is today. Taylor always makes an effort to show her appreciation through personal gestures and interactions. Her fans are a vital part of her journey. She considers them more like friends and family.

101
HORSEBACK RIDER

Taylor has shared that her mom had aspirations for her to be a horseback rider. Because of that, Taylor rode competitively until she was 12 years old. After a while, she told her mom she didn't share her passion.

TAYLOR TRIVIA

1. What is Taylor Swift's middle name?
a) Allison
b) Elizabeth
c) Marie
d) Anne

2. Where was Taylor Swift born?
a) Los Angeles, California
b) Reading, Pennsylvania
c) Nashville, Tennessee
d) New York, New York

3. What is Taylor Swift's lucky number?
a) 7
b) 10
c) 13
d) 22

4. What was Taylor's first single called?
a) "Teardrops on My Guitar"
b) "Our Song"
c) "Love Story"
d) "Tim McGraw"

5. Which album is "Shake It Off" from?
a) "Red"
b) "1989"
c) "Speak Now"
d) "Fearless"

6. Which of Taylor's cats is named after a character from "Grey's Anatomy"?
a) Olivia Benson
b) Meredith Grey
c) Benjamin Button
d) Swiftie

7. What was the first album Taylor Swift released?
a) "Fearless"
b) "Red"
c) "Taylor Swift"
d) "Speak Now"

8. In what year did Taylor Swift release "Fearless"?
a) 2006
b) 2008
c) 2010
d) 2012

9. What is the name of Taylor Swift's 2020 surprise album?
a) "Lover"
b) "Folklore"
c) "1989"
d) "Evermore"

10. Which song is known for the lyrics "We are never ever ever getting back together"?
a) "Red"
b) "I Knew You Were Trouble"
c) "We Are Never Ever Getting Back Together"
d) "22"

11. Taylor Swift made her acting debut in which film?
a) "Valentine's Day"
b) "Cats"
c) "The Giver"
d) "The Lorax"

12. What genre was Taylor's first album primarily considered?
a) Pop
b) Country
c) Rock
d) Hip-Hop

13. Which music video features Taylor as a ballerina?
a) "Love Story"
b) "Shake It Off"
c) "Blank Space"
d) "Bad Blood"

14. In which song does Taylor Swift sing about her high school crush Drew?
a) "Our Song"
b) "Fifteen"
c) "Teardrops on My Guitar"
d) "You Belong with Me"

15. Which album did Taylor win her first Album of the Year Grammy for?
a) "Red"
b) "1989"
c) "Fearless"
d) "Speak Now"

16. What is the name of the character Taylor voiced in "The Lorax"?
a) Audrey
b) Cindy Lou
c) Betty
d) Violet

17. Which album features the song "Love Story"?
a) "Speak Now"
b) "Fearless"
c) "Red"
d) "1989"

18. What is the title of Taylor Swift's second album?
a) "Speak Now"
b) "1989"
c) "Fearless"
d) "Red"

19. Which artist did Taylor collaborate with on the song "Everything Has Changed"?
a) Ed Sheeran
b) Justin Bieber
c) Shawn Mendes
d) Zayn Malik

20. Taylor Swift won her first Grammy Award for which song?
a) "Teardrops on My Guitar"
b) "You Belong with Me"
c) "Mean"
d) "Love Story"

21. What year did Taylor release her album "Red"?
a) 2008
b) 2010
c) 2012
d) 2014

22. Taylor Swift transitioned to a more pop sound with which album?
a) "Red"
b) "Speak Now"
c) "1989"
d) "Fearless"

23. Which song is known for the lyric "Darling I'm a nightmare dressed like a daydream"?
a) "Style"
b) "Blank Space"
c) "Bad Blood"
d) "Wildest Dreams"

24. What is Taylor's mother's name?
a) Andrea
b) Amanda
c) Anna
d) Alice

25. Taylor Swift's album "1989" is named after what?
a) Her favorite year
b) Her birth year
c) A famous address
d) A historical event

26. What song did Taylor Swift write for the movie "The Hunger Games"?
a) "Safe & Sound"
b) "Eyes Open"
c) "Sweeter Than Fiction"
d) "I Don't Wanna Live Forever"

27. Which song features the lyrics "You can see that I've been crying"?
a) "Teardrops on My Guitar"
b) "All Too Well"
c) "Back to December"
d) "Begin Again"

28. In which song does Taylor Swift mention her friend Abigail?
a) "22"
b) "Fifteen"
c) "Mine"
d) "Tim McGraw"

29. Taylor Swift's cat Olivia Benson is named after a character from which TV show?
a) "Grey's Anatomy"
b) "Law & Order: SVU"
c) "Friends"
d) "The Office"

30. Which song did Taylor Swift write with Max Martin and Shellback?
a) "Love Story"
b) "I Knew You Were Trouble"
c) "Our Song"
d) "Mine"

31. Which album includes the song "You Belong with Me"?
a) "Fearless"
b) "Red"
c) "Speak Now"
d) "1989"

32. Taylor Swift played a rebellious teen in which TV show?
a) "CSI: Crime Scene Investigation"
b) "NCIS"
c) "Law & Order"
d) "Grey's Anatomy"

33. Which album is known for the song "We Are Never Ever Getting Back Together"?
a) "1989"
b) "Red"
c) "Fearless"
d) "Speak Now"

34. What is Taylor Swift's younger brother's name?
a) Austin
b) Aaron
c) Andrew
d) Adam

35. In which music video does Taylor Swift play multiple characters?
a) "You Belong with Me"
b) "Blank Space"
c) "Look What You Made Me Do"
d) "Bad Blood"

36. Taylor Swift's first album was released in which year?
a) 2004
b) 2006
c) 2008
d) 2010

37. Which song features the lyrics "I remember it all too well"?
a) "Teardrops on My Guitar"
b) "All Too Well"
c) "Back to December"
d) "Begin Again"

38. Taylor Swift's "Speak Now" album was released in which year?
a) 2008
b) 2010
c) 2012
d) 2014

39. Which song did Taylor Swift release as the lead single from "1989"?
a) "Blank Space"
b) "Shake It Off"
c) "Style"
d) "Wildest Dreams"

40. Taylor Swift's cat Benjamin Button is named after a character in which movie?
a) "Forrest Gump"
b) "The Curious Case of Benjamin Button"
c) "Big"
d) "The Notebook"

41. Which Taylor Swift song features the lyrics "I see sparks fly whenever you smile"?
a) "Sparks Fly"
b) "Enchanted"
c) "Ours"
d) "Mine"

42. Taylor Swift co-wrote "This Is What You Came For" under which pseudonym?
a) Nils Sjöberg
b) Nils Schober
c) Niles Jones
d) Neil Sands

43. In which song does Taylor Swift sing "I'm just gonna shake, shake, shake, shake, shake"?
a) "Shake It Off"
b) "Blank Space"
c) "Style"
d) "Out of the Woods"

44. What song did Taylor Swift write about her ex-boyfriend Joe Jonas?
a) "Back to December"
b) "Forever & Always"
c) "Last Kiss"
d) "Dear John"

45. Which song's music video features Taylor Swift in a variety of glamorous outfits, including a cheetah-print ensemble?
a) "Wildest Dreams"
b) "Blank Space"
c) "Style"
d) "Bad Blood"

46. Taylor Swift won the Grammy for Album of the Year in 2016 for which album?
a) "Red"
b) "1989"
c) "Speak Now"
d) "Fearless"

47. Which Taylor Swift song features the lyrics "You made a rebel of a careless man's careful daughter"?
a) "Love Story"
b) "Mine"
c) "Ours"
d) "Sparks Fly"

48. In what year did Taylor Swift receive the MTV Video Music Award for Best Female Video for "You Belong with Me"?
a) 2008
b) 2009
c) 2010
d) 2011

49. Taylor Swift collaborated with which artist on the song "End Game"?
a) Ed Sheeran
b) Justin Bieber
c) Shawn Mendes
d) Zayn Malik

50. What is Taylor Swift's debut single?
a) "Tim McGraw"
b) "Teardrops on My Guitar"
c) "Our Song"
d) "Picture to Burn"

Answers

1. b) Elizabeth
2. b) Reading, Pennsylvania
3. c) 13
4. d) "Tim McGraw"
5. b) "1989"
6. b) Meredith Grey
7. c) "Taylor Swift"
8. b) 2008
9. b) "Folklore"
10. c) "We Are Never Ever Getting Back Together"
11. a) "Valentine's Day"
12. b) Country
13. b) "Shake It Off"
14. c) "Teardrops on My Guitar"

15. c) "Fearless"
16. a) Audrey
17. b) "Fearless"
18. c) "Fearless"
19. a) Ed Sheeran
20. c) "Mean"
21. c) 2012
22. c) "1989"
23. b) "Blank Space"
24. a) Andrea
25. b) Her birth year
26. a) "Safe & Sound"
27. b) "All Too Well"
28. b) "Fifteen"
29. b) "Law & Order: SVU"
30. b) "I Knew You Were Trouble"
31. a) "Fearless"
32. a) "CSI: Crime Scene Investigation"
33. b) "Red"
34. a) Austin
35. c) "Look What You Made Me Do"
36. b) 2006
37. b) "All Too Well"
38. b) 2010
39. b) "Shake It Off"
40. b) "The Curious Case of Benjamin Button"
41. a) "Sparks Fly"
42. a) Nils Sjöberg
43. a) "Shake It Off"
44. b) "Forever & Always"
45. b) "Blank Space"
46. b) "1989"
47. b) "Mine"
48. b) 2009
49. a) Ed Sheeran
50. a) "Tim McGraw"

TAYLOR QUOTES

1. **"Just be yourself, there is no one better."**
   - Taylor encourages embracing individuality and authenticity.

2. **"No matter what happens in life, be good to people. Being good to people is a wonderful legacy to leave behind."**
   - Emphasizing kindness as an enduring value.

3. **"You are not the opinion of someone who doesn't know you."**
   - Highlighting the importance of self-worth and ignoring negativity from strangers.

4. **"In life, you learn lessons. And sometimes you learn them the hard way. Sometimes you learn them too late."**
   - Reflecting on the inevitability of learning and growing from experiences.

5. **"Fearless is not the absence of fear. It's not being completely unafraid. To me, fearless is having fears. Fearless is having doubts. Lots of them. To me, fearless is living in spite of those things that scare you to death."**
   - A powerful statement on courage and overcoming fears.

6. **"People haven't always been there for me but music always has."**
   - Expressing her deep connection and reliance on music.

7. **"I never want to change so much that people can't recognize me."**
   - Staying true to her roots and identity despite fame.

8. **"Anytime someone tells me that I can't do something, I want to do it more."**
   - Her determination and drive to prove doubters wrong.

9. **"I think every girl's dream is to find a bad boy at the right time when he wants to not be bad anymore."**
   - A light-hearted take on romance.

10. **"The lesson I've learned the most often in life is that you're always going to know more in the future than you know now."**
    - A reflection on continuous learning and growth.

11. **"I think the perfection of love is that it's not perfect."**
    - Her understanding of love's complexities and imperfections.

12. **"Life isn't how to survive the storm, it's about how to dance in the rain."**
    - Finding joy and resilience in challenging times.

13. **"There are two ways you can go with pain: You can let it destroy you or you can use it as fuel to drive you."**
    - Turning adversity into motivation.

14. **"You can't have a better tomorrow if you're thinking about yesterday all the time."**
    - Encouraging forward-thinking and letting go of the past.

15. **"Happiness and confidence are the prettiest things you can wear."**
    - Promoting inner beauty and self-assurance.

QUOTES ON TAYLOR

1. **"She's truly one of the greatest living artists, period."** – Jack Antonoff
   - Celebrating her artistry and impact on music.

2. **"Taylor has this power that makes people feel like they can connect with her."** – Selena Gomez
   - On her ability to relate to and engage with her fans.

3. **"Taylor Swift is an extraordinary songwriter, the like of which comes along once in a generation."** – Andrew Lloyd Webber
   - Acknowledging her exceptional songwriting talent.

4. **"Taylor Swift's music is the soundtrack to our lives."** – Ellen DeGeneres
   - Reflecting on the universal appeal and relatability of her music.

5. **"She has the ability to make every song feel like a personal story."** – Ed Sheeran
   - On her storytelling prowess in songwriting.

6. **"Taylor Swift is a genuine person who is also a genius."** – Shawn Mendes
   - Praising both her authenticity and intelligence.

7. **"There's no one in music quite like her, and there never will be."** – Katy Perry
   - Highlighting her uniqueness and irreplaceability in the music industry.

8. **"Taylor's dedication to her fans is unparalleled."** – Camila Cabello
   - Commending her commitment to her fanbase.

9. **"She's managed to evolve and stay relevant in an ever-changing industry."** – Blake Lively
   - On her ability to adapt and remain influential.

10. **"Taylor Swift is not only a star; she's an artist who's crafted a legacy."** – Aaron Dessner
   - Recognizing her enduring impact on music and culture.

11. **"Her honesty in her music has made her a voice for her generation."** – Halsey
   - On her candidness and representation of her generation's feelings.

12. **"Taylor Swift is a once-in-a-lifetime artist."** – Tim McGraw
   - Acknowledging her rare and exceptional talent.

13. **"She's not just a singer; she's a storyteller, a poet, a friend."** – Sara Bareilles
   - Highlighting her multifaceted talent and personal connection with listeners.

14. **"Her influence extends beyond music; she's a cultural icon."** – Barack Obama
   - On her broad impact on culture and society.

15. **"Taylor Swift's journey is an inspiration to artists everywhere."** – Beyoncé
   - Commending her career path as an inspirational example for others.

THE FINALE

Wow, what an amazing journey we've had learning about Taylor Swift! From her love of board games to her habit of writing lyrics on her arms during concerts, we've uncovered so many fun and fascinating facts about her life. Taylor's story shows us that with creativity, hard work, and a little bit of quirkiness, we can achieve incredible things.

We've seen how Taylor made history with her albums, decorated her home with treasured memories from her tours, and even baked pies for her neighbors. We've learned about her love for vintage vinyl records and her passion for interior design. Every fact reveals a new side of Taylor, making her even more inspiring.

As you close this book, remember that Taylor's journey started with a dream and a lot of determination. We've left the next few pages blank so you can write down and journal what your biggest lessons from Taylor Swift are. Use this space to reflect on how Taylor's journey inspires you and what dreams you want to achieve.

Thank you for joining us on this adventure through the life of Taylor Swift. We hope you've enjoyed discovering all these amazing facts. Now, go out there and make your own magic, just like Taylor!

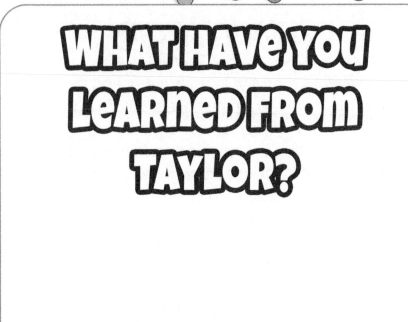

WHAT HAVE YOU LEARNED FROM TAYLOR?

Printed in Great Britain
by Amazon

44714245R00069